D0796687

Small Gods

Matthew Minicucci

New Issues Poetry & Prose

A Green Rose Book

New Issues Poetry & Prose
The College of Arts and Sciences
Western Michigan University
Kalamazoo, Michigan 49008

First Edition, 2017.

ISBN: 978-1-936970-47-6 (paperbound)

Library of Congress Cataloging-in-Publication Data:
Minicucci, Matthew.
Small Gods/Matthew Minicucci
Library of Congress Control Number: 2016919575

Editor: William Olsen
Managing Editor: Kimberly Kolbe
Layout Editor: Sarah Kidd
Assistant Editor: Ephraim Sommers
Art Direction: Nicholas Kuder
Design: Lawrence Stout
Production: Paul Sizer
                     The Design Center, Frostic School of Art
                     College of Fine Arts
                     Western Michigan University
Printing: McNaughton & Gunn, Inc.

Small Gods

Matthew Minicucci

New Issues

WESTERN MICHIGAN UNIVERSITY

Also by Matthew Minicucci

Translation

For Elizabeth

Contents

I had heard whispers of you
but now see you clearly;
therefore I will be quiet,
comforted that I am dust.
—Job 42: 5–6

One

Paul's Letter to the Romans

What if I told you desire is something with lips. Something ancient, cavernous and filled with tepid water—transparent, eyeless fish. What if it wasn't skin, or its lack, that pushed you away. What if loss was something more than your bronze gods, porcine and bright, the stink of some world hanging off the end of a spear. What if I could offer you Doubt's long sands: burnt temple; a body lost to the sap of trees. What if the small flash of emptiness at the back of the knee fired the heart of this king—this graceful thing—and each time you approached there was given love like an oil lamp. What if less, or fewer, or nothing could be augured and birds were, next to Him, the closest thing. What if no flesh was asked for, except this, this, and this night caught in the belly that bore it. What if, all this time, you were already home. What would you be willing to burn to light it?

Weeping Beech

Listen, my father
says: what a penknife

love is. But it's not
what you think. Here

we have only the hollow
of a tree, large enough

for a man's body. Or,
perhaps, the bodies

of men that so often
seek such soft places.

Often, it's pendulous
weeping that covers

the trunk. Often,
when visible, the wood

is pocked by graffiti. Such
is the nature of the inflicted

wound. Such is the two
hundred years we might

have, if undisturbed.
Nothing but the silence

of an umbrella's canopy;
dark of soft-spined husks.

Psalms

The window was closed, so no need for the sun-dipped slip into night. Plastic shade takes the place of this simple lip of sky. No lie, I saw every last minute of it; the shaky, hand-held lens in the burning throat of it. And then she swallowed, and birds like smokestacks seemed to suck into every engine we built; every light like signal flare, useless against the blues, and blacks, and this overwhelming lack. So what if the hum echoes in sleep like broken glass swept from the concrete? So what. Wait, and watch as eyes find this cradle and sway with blinked flesh, a mother's cupped breast, far above the empty fountains of winter.

Wedding

It's a shame about the fountains
in winter, the slow broken
glass of sleep, how inept quiet
can be. Sometimes it's just
the attempt that matters, how
you cross your legs at the knee
and ankle, how the priest sung
whatever words needed to be most
holy; the doxology, how the tabernacle
door slides closed like some gilded
impossible hotel. *Read Aurelius*
I said, when pressed, though he killed
his kind. That's what he called them:
kind. I said Aquinas didn't seem to mind.
For him, words meant more
than actions, or small gestures: my
head resting on your shoulder, how
close to a kiss, how uninterrupted this
dance, save for some family member's
sudden hands, nearly flush against
your dress as she whispered
it just seems like you're thinking
about what might have been.

Paul's Letter to the Corinthians

On resurrection: to the dead, the living seem so pointlessly busy.
Tireseus would agree. So concerned with the planting of seedling
trees; how water is no place of rest for horses. Or how a kettle of
hawks—away from the solitary hunt—rise together, wanting to be
reminded of just how small everything once was. My world began
as a mustard seed; nothing less than the humility of staring into the
sun. I was a horseman and then that beast of burden was removed
from me. Blindness, some bitter glass, darkly, filled with black earth.
The fear that light might only be within, or lost beneath a candle's
douter. You ask me: what is heaven? I answer with a keratitis eye
the only way to understand a place of clouds—last trump igniting
some long-standing wave that wakes the dead. Aperture and
embouchure of the living word. Speak, friends, if your mouths have
tongues. Argue there is nothing more infallible than noise.

The Body

Sometimes you put it aside. The body
I mean. Sometimes ignored the way

you stumble through a grove of trees.
But that's a lie. There are no trees here. No

giant Sequoia. No unglaciated ridges
or valleys. I often lie to you. I've often

said that I understood what you've
offered to a conversation; nodded

in agreement. Really, I've heard nothing
and this reminds me most of wind. I wish

I could tell you why. Maybe it's all better
that way: as wind. Maybe I'm a sail, or

just its luff. Or nothing at all. What I mean
to say is, perhaps, I'm most like my grandfather

who fell in the shower yesterday, in the home
he's forced to live in. And pulled the cord

that lines the floor of every room in those
sorts of homes. And of course they tell us

he'll be fine. *Fine*. Is what they say. And he
tells us nothing at all. Because perhaps

there is nothing to tell. Perhaps there's nothing
but wind, and that's why it's all he can ever hear.

Lamentations

Rodent, lilac, rhododendron. Moth sneaks its path, not flutter but fold. This better place; this light bulb forest smack in streams' forked tumble. And now, reflection in windows' storm; thunder glass; thunder that. What if touch to fingertip language. What if dust to gold alchemical. What if; what if; what if. The metal's closed; it snips and snaps and clasps the broken bone. Bow, and bend in summer's dark haze; the lamp burned out; sex's tungsten wick. Lick and laugh and spent alone. What if white paper. What if atlas held by mottled maggots. The marble's bloom. Not a single mouth to chew. And mud, mud. Such room.

to lustrate

Cleanse. Let His quiet severity pass
over each knotted head of door, or man,
or lamb left out as proof of slaughter. Let

hinge and jamb stay locked in ventric
halls, grand sternocostal surfaces always
aimed at what hangs just above. Press this

atria, this chamber, this deep concavity
that contains, now, nothing. The fire's gone
to blood, or water, or smoke aspersed across

the skin. Mark now with this hyssop stem
soaked in vinegar, a thirst; a wallflower's
laciniate leaves; small blue light.

Paul's Letter to the Corinthians (2)

There's a reason Greek has a vocative case: any thorn in flesh you can find; rocks pitted against high tide. You decide, then mind the pits, poison, or bitter taste of the olive's uncured flesh. A metaphor, perhaps, and to be expected, or expunged depending on the context. It's not that fruit isn't possible at this moment, it's just unlikely. Perhaps winter. Perhaps a blight of unknown origins: pathogenic organism; the blind white chlorosis of fungi. I don't mean to explain these things. I stand only as a farmer of men. My path took roads with no soil to speak of, so I leave this tree with you. My chains keep me here, rooted, a moment blind. Forgive this crude hand. It speaks only in looped alphas, or alephs—if we must—which always seem to find the day's last, silent light.

to flense

This part of you has a name:
integument. I prefer facsimile

of a smile; cut flesh that shows
the baleen's bend. Whalebone, however thrown

about by open mouths, can mean
so many pieces. Such bleached variety

in the wind, where even the stones go blank, sleep,
struggle along breath that escapes

like steam to cold stream above
the deck. There it hangs, brief, in

wonder; pondering whether to drop, to die
in the sea—or keep silent, endure

on as if *haar*, or sea fret, or simple
stratus, unhinged, come to earth.

Proverbs

Let's not talk about how much has been left on the porch, the rocks in the vase, the case made each day, no better with time. In rhyme, I always hate myself: drowning in a shallow pool, just to be thought a fool. Again. Fooled, of course, in the long dark spool of night. Consider how a hand brushes against another and how that is almost nothing. This morning, a cat walks carefully through the white yard, unsure of each step and yes, she reminds me of you; I want to take her in. Eat this, the body says, and stay. In the end, any breath left is wasted so let me be clear: tracks in the snow indicate at least some life, and this is intimate; how what's empty is always cavernous, no matter how delicately placed.

Paul's Letter to the Galatians

It all depends, of course, on how you define betrayal. For some, rock slips beneath, and the world tumbles from temple to new moon. Such foolish distinctions in the diction of our wounds: scratches on some tablet of clay—blinded retinal day. Let's not pretend we haven't heard the morning cry of this fleeting bird; a solemn thing. It licks the sky. It does not wonder why sand seems so much like home. Instead it only sees land like lovers' hands—arms draped in half-knots—how shape changes the story. Remember: faith is always a place we wash up on weary, and without our weapons. In the end, it's hope that brought us here.

Two

Alpha

First, the moon. Then, the rest.

The first day, unclear. Each day after, selenic; nothing but oceans and craters. Sidereal days; synodic nights. The world quartered by distant stars. Ours was a history of apparent size; lying to the sky. A history of light, reflected. History nothing but the voiced bilabial plosive. By which I mean: the voice tract occlusive; all airflow ceased. By which I mean: I don't know what to say.

For any two variables, we can estimate the change and relationships between. You called this regression: linear and simple. I called it the steps to your apartment. The locked door. How exchanged glances become the barycenter of balanced and balancing bodies.

The truth is, a first morning together is always multinomial: such discrete possible outcomes. Perhaps it's only supposed to be a moment; all just aleatory in the end. Perhaps it's about how you decide to partition the probability space of an egg, double-yolk, sunny-side up. What you might call the problem of two bodies; but what I named the tide.

Gamma

Elementary, really, if we're talking about light.
Complex, if it's numbers or you. It seems we're
always talking about you. Eventually, there are
deviations from standard behavior: a cat wandering
the yard, ripped groundcover, the specific weight of
each sungold you forgot to pick. Microscopic
interactions lost in simple concentrations, partial
pressures.

Everything changes with time. And speed changes
time. And maybe everything is an object if that
object is moving. By which I mean my hand against
yours during the long spindle of sleep. A continuum
of cotton; the shear deformation of parallel surfaces
sliding past one another.

Easy metaphors like tectonic plates torsioned.
Circulation lost in my arm beneath your hair,
shorter now: reflection as length squared divided by
time, impedance discontinuity as related to this
messy shared medium. There is some light left, on
the surface. A different index of refraction, you
might say. And I might say *summer is over.* Or,
entropy increases in an isolated system. Or, nothing
at all.

Small, or uncertainly so. Mouth of this. Tributary of that. Tribute can be a small copper coin in a small copper bowl; gold, if you're lucky, or blessed, or considerate of either. The sound against metal registers as infinitesimal among the infinitesimal changes in a closed system. The act of giving: continuous, but irrelevant.

Of course it means the striped back of a moth against the morning newspaper; the single wing that struggles to begin. Of course there's a tiny hole in the Tatsoi. Everything eats. Everything deflects under a heavy load, like a cantilever beam given a new radian angle. Here is my fixed end. Here is my free. A show of force multiplied by some length cubed.

It's a poem of force, or force that indents this cross-beam into the inflammation of a mosquito bite. It hurts? Say three *Hail Marys*, and use force if it bothers you again. Remember: though you are the defendant, and He is the prosecutor, the burden of proof is yours.

Epsilon

Elektron. Amber. Drawstring and light bodies, left without scratch or stitch from a needle. *Ad* or *ab*, depending on the oscillation of this swing. Dynamic. Direction just formed; the production of some length: arbitrarily small, insignificantly distant. For example: the empty space between fathers and sons. The permittivity of a straw-grass cow-lick when reached for; resistance encountered there.

The nature of this sort of family is deformation: displacement of bodies; distance of relative particles to relative particles. Their interactions only a deflection of light, sum of the squared differences between place where and time since.

In the end, all we consider is what can be held in the palm like a silver coin; an uncle's favorite parlor trick. The not-so-bright star of this backyard constellation set against the world like a pall. How well we absorb the flash at a given wavelength. How elastic these easy smiles can be.

Zeta

Vorticity. Any city, really, where trees curl in sucked
smoke. The street artist's tendency to spin within a
fluid stroke; the circular breath of *geese, weasel,
well*. Standard models for a Sunday. Rigid rotational
axis. Potentially, all of this is merely colloidal:
substance perfectly distributed in substance;
dispersal hidden within the continuous.

Damp today, and everything decays after a brief
disturbance. Whip tick oak leaves suck against wire
fence like shrimp to baleen teeth. Struggle and bail.
Struggle and bale. Oscillations of a tin spring life:
parameters of loss, hidden sway of steel girder
babel; the largely hypothetical equality.

This stigma carries no weight here. Values bound
by ligature only; the connections we form in sixty
watts of cursive light. Our newspapers lack
diagammas. The names there only acrophonic.
Front-page editorial: we've all become so diacritical.

Eta

Lately, distance travelled; a lone observer and the
long, gray age of the universe. There is a maximum
space between you and the bedside lamp, unlit. For
every particle and particular light, Y is true. Y could
be some boundary, undefined, between the canoed
curves in the bed; unobservable regions; space as
entirely conformal: all the angles right; all these
distances distorted.

Leaving, you argued the value of a neutral axis: how
there must, mathematically, be a place where no
strain exists. Another day, it seems, another bright
star. Electrons per photon; amps per watt. The
kindness of thermodynamics: how each system is a
state; each state only one in a cycle; each cycle
returning finally to an initial condition. Or some
such nonsense.

I'm sure I wasn't listening, lost in elasticity; response
observed in one variable as defined by the change in
another. Gradient decrease in the inevitable passing
of this to that. Sometimes each set seen only in
adjunction: spoken word on the non-essential
attribute of a thing. How the lamp still sits there;
how it hasn't worked for days.

Theta

For her, the garden as a special function of many complex variables. Potential temperatures. Population mutation rates. Dirt tracked into the threshold of this antechamber or that. Anger as an ordinal number: *how many times have I fucking said* this house is a collapsing function. I know. There just wasn't enough water for the trestled cucumbers; summer hanging on in its slack and dimensionless heat.

You ask when the arguments began to tend towards the space between this particular value and infinity and to this, I have no response. Once, we performed simpler functions within our asymptotic algorithms: testing limits; closeness to the line as an arbitrary aspect of my twin bed, value in each angle squared.

Perhaps we just end the story because we must, without proof, only inference of affection; the likelihood of sex within the parameters of any incomplete model: wounded; bound by nothing more than what was once a skylight with all its gentle and genitive light. The almost archaic form your mouth made when you used to swallow the sky.

Iota

What if silence was the smallest unit of measure for distance between two people. An imaginary number. A defining equation with two distinct solutions, equally valid. What if I began the poem again, started this time with quiet instead. What if quiet was the smallest unit of measure for distance between a man and a woman sitting together at the end of an unfinished bench, the edge of this world, wanting for nothing.

But no. You and your uniqueness quantification. You and your *there is one and only one*. I get the logic. I understand. To prove the existence of a particular thing A, with all its desire and desired qualities, you assume the existence of another thing B, and deduce their equality.

Simple: start with the transitive property. Pass over these things. End, of course, with cancellation. Always an inevitable sum. Unmistakable equality. Proof held in the backyard's topological space where two continuous functions won't speak to one another. Not when there's so much to see: dashed line of a fence, just enough space to bury any number of things.

Kappa

It's raining again, you say. Near flow and no-slip. Car on the curvature of space and time and boxed wine. Here: the clear empty well of a disappointed glance. New glacier. Gravitation and some brief disturbance of cohabitation. Volume as a function of change in pressure and stress. *What a fucking mess.*

By which I mean these voices long-gravelled. By which I mean a singular sort of silence caught in the distribution of moments: steel fixed joint; live load at an adjacent point. All of it indeed a moving, variable weight.

Factor this, solve for that. Say for any cardinal along the road, Z is true. Z might be number of beats possible by each wing divided by miles not migrated. Or how it's always a sad, sad distance to one special, sharp-crested mate; that tiny brown sweater she always likes to wear in winter.

Lemma

Open mouth, or shadow, or nothing of the sort.
The retort is exactly like a flooded road: unusable;
disappointment in all the directions we fail to go.
Or know. Let me tell you about the train, how it
rises above everything in this town. How we kneel
beneath its animated corpse. If wheels, then move.
If a sign, then perch, hawk.

These are just the tenants of a thing, this place, a
lemma for the way you wear your hair; your
intentions; the fingerless gloves of winter. So much
uncovered, so much technical, or jargon, or the
placement of pots on a stove; the wine that sits
open until closed. A gift: the logic of riding downhill
in a place with no hills. We pretend.

We place this scenery where we see fit: call
another to the stage, explain the arc as closed,
differentiable, and fallen. Hands are all that's left to
support the eye's foundation. How barefoot, speed
seems a functionality of faith. I have so little in my
shirt pocket. So few letters to name the street lamps.
They are replaced, improved, like all things.
Somewhere, unnamed fires still burn like Pentecostal
hair, or grieving soldiers so utterly undone.

Lambda

Bright. Vinegar bright. Windows until no windows remain. Each knitted cap slowly falling away like leather-strapped shields on tired arms. There is no neighborhood here. No gravity but the minor movement of key chains; their dangling planetesimals.

Tell me the story of the island made of glass: how it blinded each inhabitant. How little they once thought of loss. How they still polished each panel. Tell me that celestial navigation is caught in this lens flare; how much radiation makes up cold and breath and the fountain that seems to pull water from its mouth like stitches. Tell me about the action potential of this rolling paint job and the exponential rate of decay in every brief look.

There can only be one null string. Every other block spits symbols like a boxer into a bucket. The truth is: light behaves differently depending on direction, time, and the material reflecting. *You'll see a mirror without its right or left corner, depending on the day*, the janitor says. *Sometimes, we just can't stand what little is left.*

Mu

Orbital mechanics, really. The motion of this body, any body to the constant pull of the George Washington Bridge, its star-lit tollbooths. On the Henry Hudson parkway, dead leaves move like lost children. Reluctantly they share the stale air. For all elementary particles, X is true. X is most likely decay, or the loneliness of separation from this atomic life.

It's natural to find yourself in the background radiation, or to understand relativistic speeds in New York traffic. The exit ramp considers the nature of a single dimension. I consider the narrow chain of cars pulled through city parks like kite string. In linguistics, *mora* is a single unit of syllabic weight. I consider yelling at the yellow cab to add more syllabic weight to my overall point. I remind him that *mora* has no etymological relationship to *mores*, our simple ways, or virtues, or values.

The small man has no *mores*. I think, perhaps, I can handle no more. The woman at the tollbooth takes my small change, and my large bills. She licks her fingers as she counts each folded corner. She stares at me as if I were her one-millionth customer.

Freedom, or fission. Or both, of course. Of course,
of course, of course. It varies, to some degree.
Distributions arise. How to part with this; parry
that. How to calculate the number of dimensions in
this domain. You say variance and I say divergent.
And then we say nothing at all.

Perhaps connection is periodic: a sine wave
oscillating in some smooth repetitive pattern. Wake,
sleep, deep water. Wake, sleep, deep water. Inertia
is resistance, first, before all other things, but we
know this. I've said it a thousand times. Do I have
to say it again? Volatility. Sensitivity. Derivative of
the option value with respect to the underlying
asset.

A door, for example, how it's not a true anomaly.
How it swings open in the summer, in even the
smallest amount of wind. Precipitation and
reaction. The periapsis of a sun-dress wandering
around the house, picking lemon mint. A confession:
I've never understood celestial mechanics. A
corollary: the door; I never fixed it.

The air polytropic; this formula like a fish swimming in any spherically symmetrical fluid. What if random variables. What if we let X equal this small arm that sweeps this snow from a thin plastic sled, or the frequency at which one hears a voice descend the mountain; just how long it takes to climb back up again.

Perhaps all of this is a complex number, or the argument made by the rosacea that paints late afternoon trees. What's certain: there's a moon here built of bailing twine. Some impossible moon. Separation of galaxies as measured in the median's tire tracks; a correlative function of gravel to salt to gravel to snow to boot.

Here: a man moves logarithmically: all base and fixed values. He knows it's only sledding down a hill, with his daughter. That it's only the small hat he once wore as a boy; or the tree that took his first splintered bone. But this place is a paradox; a universal set. Steps, all some distinct and definite object, each containing both itself and all other things.

Omicron

We don't talk about it, but there's an order of operations to leaving: calculate, divide, deal with the variables; taping the bottom of each box before the top. Of course. Of course, it's all just random, which side we choose. Just where we decide to make our mark. We're foolish, you and I, and we do foolish things.

When you told me about him, foolish him, I could only respond in the vocative: *Oh. Oh. Oh.* Oh mikron. Oh mega. The smallest of things, and the biggest. The furthest star in a constellation group is still brighter than anything you've ever imagined, but is only punctuation to the sky. Giant, fiery, and ancient punctuation.

Eventually, perhaps inevitably, we arbitrarily approach the limit of this function. We can try to find where there's still growth, *if and only if there exist positive numbers*. But we both know the argument is tending toward infinity; all simpler functions seem spent. Sufficiently large. Suitably close. It seems, once again, we're left with X.

Pi

At some point, you just stop counting.

Rho

It starts with talk of constants: an iris of standing water; climbing bittersweet; maidenhair and the long rolling fog of ivy. She climbs stairs to nowhere and continues on despite. Here, her two fingers press against the green snowflake of a rattlesnake fern; skin along the spark of each frond.

There's talk of resistance on Belle Isle. Every whisper is measured in ohms. Each hope is lost in the white froth and stone oculi of the James River. This place is a brief half-life: all hadrons, despite how stout they might be, fall away. Old Dominion Iron and Steel remains as a single brick wall; a hollow doorway only to itself. Quarrymen lost granite to the river eventually, their pickaxes useless against the water's spitting heads. The idyllic scene rendered only because of perfect tension and retention.

Her father understands this. He knows of a place where sky and water are the same thing. It exists only in each coulomb of electrical charge in his laptop; the integration of scene to scene to scene. But these beautiful renderings become dependent on one another; no longer random variables of sun to bough, or the encroaching lip of river strung like a bow. *Look*, he says, *I can make an oil painting of the world. With one click I can smooth away every bristled trichome.*

Sigma

This life, like the plight of just-planted trees, where everything begins in the bed of a truck. From there, a hope for dirt: regolith religion; the unknown angle at the alley's blind corner. Such concern for a world out of position, wandering, the velocity dispersion of some family's globular cluster.

Of course dust is spun out from the center. Of course. Such debts and demands resist balance. And the sum of these things sits on surface tension; how water loves water more than air. And by this I mean everyone leaves, eventually, if only for the nearest hotel: force per unit length; energy per unit area.

Such terrible kindness in instruction; simple plans with sharp edges; how a boy learns: fat storage; flight mechanics; an envelope with no letter. Pathology as evidenced by a ripped magazine cover reminding us that everything will someday burn in endless summer; red corona of a sad, old sun.

Difficult, but not to be confused with *wound*, or *mark*, or the sharp twist in the road ahead. If one said *curve*, there might be some tension lost: how the headlights can nearly penetrate the opacity of this storm; how the clouds linger and sway, as if unswept. Bayer never had the chance to name this road. He might have called it *first among equals*, or *last*. All in Greek, of course. He may have known that when you mention twins, whether in constellations or in the hollow hull of a black ship, Castor always precedes.

Bollocks to Pollux. Everyone pays attention to his brother: the horseman, the athlete. Everyone pays attention to his sister: the whore, the *lacrimae*. When someone inevitably asks, they say *half immortal, thank you*. Which is to say not entirely divine and not entirely held in the black dirt, the long banks, the cut corn that lie like spent sheaths and scabbards.

What happens to an animal when it's kept in complete darkness? Forget this face. Forget your place, brother. Forget the lance of each lament; the tortuosity of finger felt walls. Movement requires mass, then weight, then faith in guided closure of object from position to place. In the beginning, a hand is held above the head. It rests in anticipation of arc. Its aim always just beyond whatever it seeks to destroy.

Upsilon

Regarding this apartment's spatial volume: too much mass, not enough luminosity. By which I mean, the porch light was out when I got back. By which I mean, you weren't there. No need for photometry to measure that flux. Maybe all this time you were the trapped standing wave. Sure, I can give you that. Maybe, in the end, it was always about boundary conditions.

Did you know that some insignificant matter between a distant source and a sole observer can bend light itself? This is not a metaphor. To the observer, that light would look so much like a ring, all fucking axially symmetrical. This is, again, not a metaphor.

Maybe misalignment. Maybe just an arc segment, as it turns out. Maybe every word you said to me about him set in my skin like a secant line; cut like its Latin root. Or, maybe I lied. Maybe that matter between some distant source and this sole observer is significant after all. Maybe it's massive. Maybe it's some mass M, at some distance r, where G is the universal constant of gravitation, c the speed of light, and I, well, I'm torn, like time itself.

Phi

Easy, like always: lax latitude and roll angle. Just some damn geodesy. In the end, we were always about pressure: real divided by the ideal. Characteristic function; normal distribution. The predicate logic of a yard's paper birch. For example: for each yellow horned lark, there exists a pennyworth piece of bark. Simple.

But I did not tell you this. Instead, I remembered just how important prepositions are: closest to; furthest from. Don't worry, it isn't just us. Every kind of science measures the void eventually; here is just our particular porosity.

The truth is: I never know what to say to the sky. Irreducible sun. Roots and their complex union; sad, mislaid multiplicative identity. This cardinal number. That ordinal street. When you called, you made leaving sound as generic as flying. *Look, people do it all the time.* But what if, all this time, flying was just falling towards something else. What if they lied to us. People do it all the time.

Chi

What if two specific lines of equal length again cross? Crossing again, as equals, those long specific lines at a single point. If you'd listen. If what you've said can be heard. Finally. A bird, of course, could be a perfect image for our battle standards. What I might call a *vexillum*, but what you see in the backyard's papilionaceous plants.

Because you seem so much like a butterfly now. By which I mean only this chaplet of wings you've just begun to grow. Such belief in Bernoulli's principle: increasing speed reduces pressure. Even at the loss of all the possible potential energy in this system.

In the end, you said *simple* and I said *inviscid*. And then, as always, we said nothing at all. You just left, one day, and I didn't stop you because this silence seemed ideal. As open as an empty hallway that still remembers your voice as I run the vacuum one more time.

Psi

The body branches like fire: entirely un-random, as rain falls outside rooms of light and less than light. Fluid mechanics and flow velocity; how water is always trying to leave. The dark seemed to suggest what all this could be: a window; a yard's tree; lock that might unlatch. Sparks, then you, then you again.

Perhaps, in the end, I'll be swept up like all things. Again, in the curve of her back. Then again, everything is swept away, she says. No perhaps. She says *wind*. She says *sweat* and *sweet* and *shudder*. The thing that turns and so begins again. Bough split in gravity's heavy hands. Data from datum. A body's dihedral angles.

And then, tangent sleep. The circadian clarity of shadow to a cross-beam. Gesture as recursion. Of course it only appears vast, like the sea. How you could swear it remembered us; how surprised we are not to be forgotten.

The end, Janus-faced cliché. The eschatology of a
door. Hinge-pin rolling across the floor, lost to a
solid angle subtended. Or the multiplicity of moving
furniture; microstates uncertain in a living room's
dusty system. Boxes stacked, waiting to be filled:
object, object, subobject. So much like bodies
intertwined, you say. How one always fits inside
another.

But maybe you say none of this. Maybe what's left
is just some turbulent apology: topology; the
perceived properties of space preserved. When
there's turbulence, there's also a specific rate of
dissipation; pressure changing with respect to time.

For example: how a parcel of air seems to traverse
the space between two open windows without
incident. Such streamlines & streaklines &
pathlines; probability that any randomly constructed
program will suddenly halt. High-energy; short
lived. The simple division of a last night together.
How for every number N there are X prime factors
that divide the integer exactly. How you could see
them when you closed your eyes, branching like
beetroot. How you told me you can dream of
nothing else.

Proof

There's little of the nothing to be said. And yet. And yet again. Proof, with its symbols and parenthetical statements like a scored seed; plant that hugs the stone wall. To have shadow, you need light and a lack of light. This is not important.

He believes these beautiful things. A young boy climbs the hill next to them. The boy doesn't speak, only watches with eyes that seem to grab at the man's beard like tiny fingers. It's the red of stonecrop man dreams it will be white someday. This is about pigment: the carbon filling the water in ink; the body which has no ink at all. This is what the body is: soft, the curve of the iliac crest; the tiny brown leaf above her nipple.

There's nothing written about the end: the arc of this wave settles and is settled. For the moment, it seems water is only cut glass: a brief sketch etched. He wonders how close to the heart the knife goes; what happens to each discarded sliver.

Three

Paul's Letter to the Ephesians

Consider: the stars held out to a man in chains—like amaranth flowers—like the night turned unfading red. Simple dyes that could light this heart. Portends to the jailer; auspice to the prisoner who dreams of a long, calm sea. In the end, we both—jailer and jailed alike—see the boat launched from shore set aflame. You, my friends, might seek to augur with any viscera you find: an ibis exsanguinated; the lump in your throat. Or throw stones at this moon like the half-open eye of a lover, teasing you. Understand, though, all meals are last when eaten with something better in mind. What, you ask? Whispered prayer, perhaps, like a small brass key. Or that iron manacles and fetters mean nothing to a forge.

Black Ship, Swept

When my grandfather says
    then, my ship will be gone, I have no response.

    And so

    I mourn, just as my mother
        taught me to do. Just as she was taught

by her mother, and each mother before that: a clew
    held taut, as when I said *I miss you*

    and to this

    you had no response. Only that the *ship*
        has been swept, swept, swept

sweeps away, I know but I do not know what
    to say. What I'm looking for is here by the coffee and cornflakes

    always, that there is

    another cave, lit but still
        dark like remains, or

the simple inertia of a swaying body sculpted
    to simulacra from ashes,

    as if

    by a mother's heavy
        hands.

Small Gods

Consider the wisp of jellyfish. Lion's mane; box. Consider
    the swarm; the bloom. Consider the ocular individual
        reaching, even after death, toward vacating shores.

What we know as one being began as an ancient
    many. The eldest of the organed things. The organs once
        beings themselves; huddled in the pulsating bell; coiled

in this medusozoan catch. The beings now being, singular.
    The once breathtaking migratory patterns along the ocean's flyway;
        the turn and dips; the sacred and supple shapes of the sea; now held

within this hydrostatic shell, soft, specialized
    as manubrium or velarium, like so much
        stitched awning. Consider the movement

to light, slow and surfacing. The tropism
    of the life cycle's cycling many. Consider
        the sacrifice; evolution's creeping mesoglean walls.

Remember that between the fibrous proteins, the collagens
    of the keep, there is mostly water; so much so that, to them,
        the body's prison is no more cold or dark than the rest.

From the Rising

This distance, only flecks and flecks. Only
a slow build. No barrel vaulted arch and its lateral
forces; no gleaming firmament in His ancient eyes.
What's said is sadness builds like strata:

significance mapped on the back of a hawksbill turtle.

At night, the stars were engulfed in fire; in themselves.
Through thigmotropic eyes, the magi found presage: broken
knucklebone; nightshade; petiole. Sleeping grass, its fruit
like viscera and blood. The body: only taxonomy. Their words

waves of alveolar consonants; the white foam of each bilabial stop.

Paul's Letter to the Philippians

About sadness, all epistles are written in Greek: the unknown angle in each *sigma*; how the *alpha* always implies the missing *aleph*. Perhaps there's nothing more to say about the dark. How the night would rather be apostle to emptiness than minister to wind. Wind as that ubiquitous and hollow gift. Wind like tidal water living in the pinna of the ear. It may sing sorrow as salvation's undertow. Or lift blood from a stone already washed by foam. Or, it may do nothing of the sort. Now, at the end, we talk about Doubt like Thomas. Yes, blessed are those who believe without seeing. But blessed more are those who must accept the slivered hangnail of this proof when pressed deep within the cavities of their own flesh.

Heartwood

One morning a tree grew
      from the base of your spine. The long strokes
      of it; tangles of hair. Branches wrapped in
      the way our fingers knot each other, trying to

forget their lonely masters. And you opened
      your arms like fall, with the rounded bills
      of tanagers singing their way from your breasts.
      And I understood their red and black

wings. How much like passing seasons.
      How your body could only genuflect,
      canopy covering this crown, and sway
      with whatever winds the world had left.

I named them once. The winds. I tried to name you, but
      my mouth darkened like heartwood. That,
      like all things, was a kind of death. The sort
      that leaves you unarmed and lying in a field.

Paul's Letter to the Colossians

A road, once. Farther on, the dust kicked up by cloven burden. And then nothing but a glimpse of my father's face; the volume and displacement of his charges. In the void, I confess I was not strong: baptismal tears; fear like a bloomed *calanit*. Perhaps we never consider a stone, or the street it builds until we're dragged through it. Faith like sores on the knee and elbows, remembered with every brief turn. Forget where I came from, or who I smiled for. We all seek justice in some flawed way until justice comes, like heavy rain, or overgrowth embracing an abandoned *mikveh*. It's not that we've forgotten the oven or the olive press of our childhood home, it's just we can't find our way back. Somewhere, a road leads to my broken basalt and bricks. It dreams in repose.

John of Patmos

John the Seer. John the Divine. Saint
of exiles and exiled saints. The Sporades home

to the unwanted, the way an archipelago
wanders from the shore like fingers

from an open hand, dendrites that branch electrochemical
stimulation; govern the spike and swell of action potentials.

Consider the potential of a body. It can lay beneath
this olive tree. It can feel the spidery fingers of God

touch each synapse like a talon. It can be moved; enthused.

Sometimes, the body is a woman. Her hands long and flat like a panther's,
her eyes hexagonal and glittering in long sheets of mica.

Her spit is the sea. Her whine the broken
and spent husks of branch and fruit: phenolic and bitter.

Each day the sun chases her from this place. Each night
she returns to hide the rock of the world inside her.

Cairn

Incremental and sacramental, in till
and tall grass. Some shine or sound
like strophe and antistrophe; rifled: bore
and fit. A single line from this chorus
that points to ships unseen. Preparation
in deed, in decree and declined. This line
of kings lost like oars, easily broken
at length. Rows like hedge maze, each
stone this man or that placed upon another
like melancholy. Bones as boxed fertilizer.
Grief left like loam to brief the incoming
waves, foam ships, wine-dark seas.

Paul's Letter to the Thessalonians

Last night, everything. The world a shark-tumbling moon—all spiracle, spiracle, caudal fin. Again, about resurrection, I can say the Kingdom of Heaven is a glass oar: invisible in calm waters, then sharp in the swells. How the distance between trough and crest, this fetch, stands as ontological if you're the sea. And, of course, you are. Even a single voice strokes some capillary waves. So to mourn is as natural as life's given bourne. But know, in the end, that the heart of this strange creature is two-chambered. Met along some road, perhaps, in the afternoon's occluded air. We duly fall and meet His kingdom—corona of a quiet, old sun. We bask in the fire of familiar tongues.

to mordant

When the hand's perfect lines amount
    to nothing but leather, rejoice

at this brief dye lake, or lac, or shade
    left in winter's drought.

Snow of any kind would soften the bite
    on what garden is left beyond

this fence, sun gilt, pressed to protect
    rot, graveyard lit up in late

afternoon cochineal, almost crimson
    to these amphoteric eyes.

Polycarp

Known for who is known. Known for the probable known. Known and known and forgotten. Forget the fuel-to-air ratio. Forget the stab, to station, to sail. To sail again with John and John and John, and sail with wind and hail and boats unmoored. To describe: unmoored and adrift; explication and incense and incensed at *what thou wilt*. Aurelius, thou wilts, thou wanders in a strange land. Don't we all? Don't we wilt, and wander and resist the thurible that makes chains of these wings? The sacrifice therein; *thuein*; the stab or the smell. Choose. There is no tether here. Each blaspheme uttered only a possible noose. Choose. The miraculous like a breeze, passing, pulling, placing the steel; the sternum now only hull and keel. Respite. The single breath: *in principio, et nunc, et semper*. Let the wind come. Perhaps the spirit is a spritsail after all.

Willet

If possible, forgiveness
may probe, or pause, or pierce
in its return call. Straight bills
hang agape, as if some strain
to speak the words; surprise
at the rolling crustacean's empty
carapace. If possible, forgiveness
may be alone, startled, running with wings
outstretched: forgetting flight but
alight on the mudflats. If possible,
forgiveness may feign a broken
wing, caesura in the song, chase
drawn from bared teeth, the undisguised
hunger. If possible, forgiveness
would appear only overhead, call
when past, continue on
in shadow, dark shapes, rumor's
flight over mottled sand.

Paul's Letter to the Thessalonians (2)

Salvation is a missive I read backwards. How it's the beginnings that sway us—that bright birth from a many-hearted somewhere. And here, right here, it lies like an open wound: what little can be said in defense of the long night; scratched stone beneath a heavy grate. It's all just water outliving the flesh in you, or dust gathered like surfeit stars. I can show you a path if by path you mean nothing but desiccated overgrowth. You may mistrust, like all creatures, but what a joyful herd that finds one of its own, long ago thought lost to the road. Just imagine what sights it's seen—such lament in its psalms.

Whale

Flowering, from the tip of this
to the end of that. Submissive
        only to the scythe, and bright
without edge; without corners
        to be caught. A creature
unconfused by a world where
        even rock once bubbled. Because
everything bubbles; every bauble
        on this shore a fool's scepter, held
until sand wicks to sand it's briefly
        missed. This goes unnoticed in the deep,
where half-dome batholiths sit
        like sunken state parks. Without edge.
A place where air is either intrusion,
        or held willfully, precious cargo set
in lungs like vaulted cathedrals, Romanesque,
        silent until that moment where we brief
congregations file from narthex to altar,
        ushered to what might wait just above.

An Old Man, Full of Days

In the end, everything turns out
right, like the last ten verses
of Job, where rings are given
in supplication and apology. Where sheep
reappear in fields and stand bleating
next to a thousand yoke of
oxen. Where the latter days are
blessed more than the beginning. Where
even ghosts of lost children stand
exhumed by the voices of new
ones, more fair than the first.
In this ancient language, there is
one meter for heated debate and
a second for lament. There has
never been any consideration of another.

Philemon

History is a hum. You must understand. Each of us unmade by the sight of the angel's strings; dulcet beat of its wings. Every announcement only bad news, of course: a husband's ship come to port; each man to blood; a mother's blinding brooch. The ubiquitous children lost. Just story, you know. No guardian. No just juxtaposition of sorrow on stage. Story. Standing water complete with swallowtails; simple facts, unsympathetic. In time, this skin is a vellum we read. Indeed, every word a step from ship to shore, madness to men like us interred in some granite mortuary. Go. Go and tell them that here I will lie mournful. No stone in this box left unstudied; each just another cold iris for the world.

Notes

All of the poems in the "Paul's Letter to..." series are responding to the Revised Standard Edition (1952) versions of Paul's epistles. The epigraph, from the Book of Job, is also taken from this edition of the Bible.

The book's second section owes a great debt to countless textbooks and reference materials on mathematics, the natural sciences, linguistics, and astronomy. These include, though are certainly not limited to: Carl Boyer's *A History of Mathematics,* David Berlinski's *A Tour of the Calculus* and *The Advent of the Algorithm,* and Scott Birney's *Observational Astronomy.*

"*Pi*" is dedicated, with many thanks, to Zachariah McVicker.

"Black Ship, Swept" is dedicated to my grandfather, Carmine Minicucci, who passed away on June 16th, 2016.

Acknowledgments

Thanks to the journals in which the poems below previously appeared, sometimes in different versions or forms:

32 Poems: "Paul's Letter to the Ephesians," "Paul's Letter to the Thessalonians (2)"

Adroit Journal: "*to flense*"

Cumberland River Review: "*Rho*," "Paul's Letter to the Corinthians (2)," "Philemon"

Hayden's Ferry Review: "*Lambda*"

Hobart: "*Mu*," "Proof," "*Zeta*"

The Gettysburg Review: "*Gamma*," "*Iota*"

The Journal: "Polycarp," "John of Patmos"

Mid-American Review: "Lemma"

New Flash Fiction Review: "Kappa"

Quarterly West: "*Eta*," "*Theta*"

Poor Claudia: "*Beta*," "*Epsilon*," "*Nu*," "*Sigma*," "*Phi*," "*Omega*"

Prodigal: "*Chi*"

Southern Indiana Review: "*Omicron*"

Third Coast: "Paul's Letter to the Romans," "Paul's Letter to the Corinthians"

Tuesday: An Art Project: "*Upsilon*"

Virginia Quarterly Review: "An Old Man, Full of Days"

West Branch: "Paul's Letter to the Thessalonians (1)," "Lamentations"

West Branch Wired: "*Tau*," "*Delta*"

"Polycarp" was reprinted on *Verse Daily* March 22nd, 2014.

photo by Robert Hirschfeld

Matthew Minicucci is the author of one previous collection of poetry, *Translation* (Kent State University Press, 2015), chosen by Jane Hirshfield for the 2014 Wick Poetry Prize. He is the recipient of fellowships and awards from the Bread Loaf Writers' Conference, the Wick Poetry Center, and the University of Illinois at Urbana- Champaign, where he received his M.F.A. His work has appeared in numerous journals and anthologies, including *Best New Poets 2014*, *The Gettysburg Review*, *Kenyon Review*, *The Southern Review*, and the *Virginia Quarterly Review*. He currently lives in Portland, OR with his partner Elizabeth and their cat, Puck.

The Green Rose Prize